THE BIG LITTLE BOOK OF
BUTTERFLIES

THE BIG LITTLE BOOK OF BUTTERFLIES

JEFFREY GLASSBERG

Sterling Publishing Co., Inc.
New York

Published by Sterling Publishing Co., Inc.
387 Park Avenue South, New York, NY 10016

©2004 by Sterling Publishing Co., Inc.

Distributed in Canada by Sterling Publishing
c/o Canadian Manda Group, One Atlantic Avenue, Suite 105
Toronto, Ontario, Canada M6K 3E7
Distributed in Great Britain by Chrysalis Books
64 Brewery Road, London N7 9NT, England
Distributed in Australia by Capricorn Link (Australia) Pty. Ltd.
P.O. Box 704, Windsor, NSW 2756, Australia

ISBN 1-4027-1782-2

Color separations by Bright Art Graphics Singapore
Printed and bound in China by C&C Offset Printing

1 3 5 7 9 10 8 6 4 2

Contents

Introduction 6

Photographs 8

List of Plates 300

Index of Common and Scientific Names of Butterflies 311

WITH DAZZLING COLORS AND GRACEFUL FLIGHT, butterflies bring smiles to our faces and beauty to our lives. As embodiments of the human soul and as symbols of freedom, they cause us to reflect upon the impermanence of each life and upon our place in the universe. As important pollinators of flowering plants and as a food source for birds and other animals, butterflies play a central role in the ecosystems that support our civilization and serve as early warning indicators of the health of the environment. Perhaps just as important is the intense pleasure these small creatures can provide, forging a bond between human beings and the natural world. This bond nourishes our souls and spurs us to take action to conserve the living world around us.

The photographs in this book were taken in the United States, Mexico, and Europe. All were taken of wild butterflies in their natural habitats. (A large percentage of butterfly photographs seen in calendars and elsewhere are of butterflies that have been captured, cooled on ice, and then placed, immobile, on types of flowers that they would not normally visit.)

I hope that this collection of photographs sets you on the road to a lifetime involvement with butterflies and all of nature.

—Jeffrey Glassberg

To learn more about butterflies, visit the website of the North American Butterfly Association (NABA), www.naba.org.

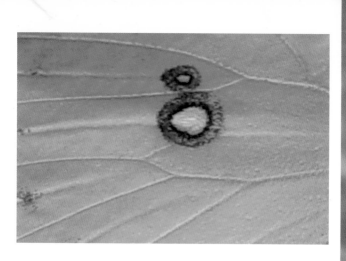

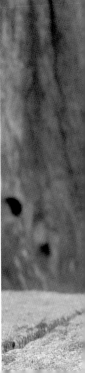

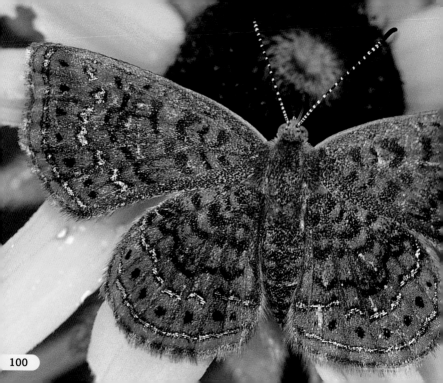

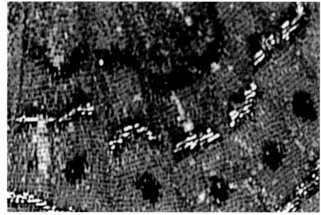

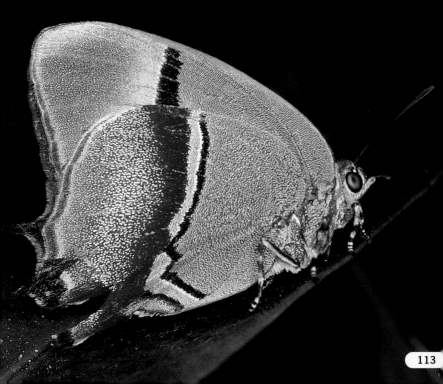

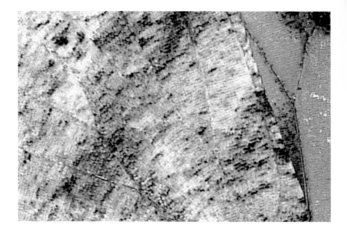

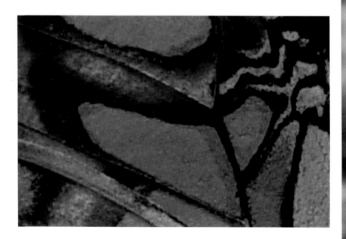

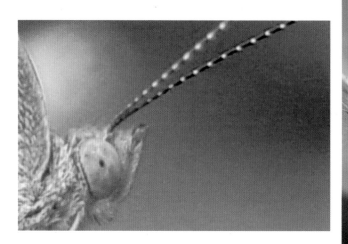

184

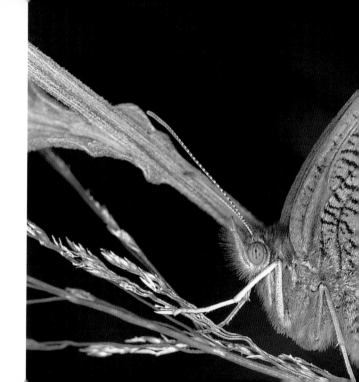

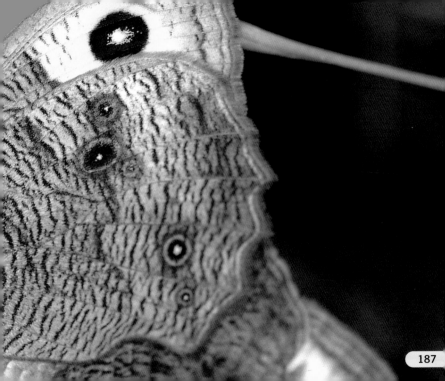

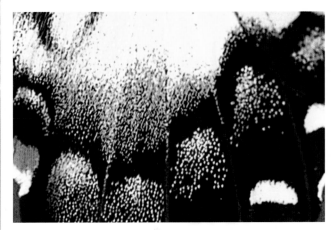

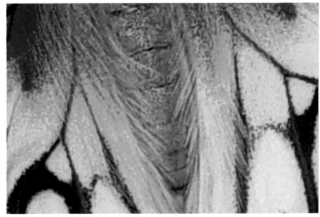

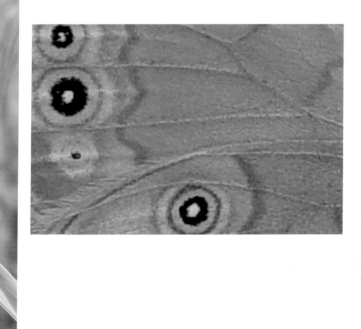

253

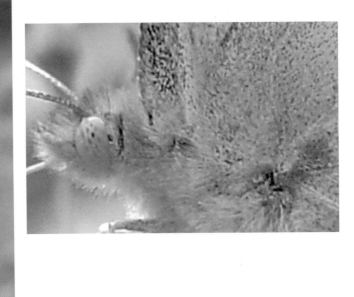

List of Plates

Location indicates where the photograph of the butterfly was taken.

Page	Butterfly: (Common Name, *Latin Name*)	Location
8	Queen, *Danaus gilippus*	Dominican Republic
9	White-rayed Pixie, *Melanis cephise*	Mexico
10, 11	Southern Dogface, *Colias cesonia*	U.S.
12	Zebra Heliconian, *Heliconius charithonia*	U.S.
13	Blue Metalmark, *Lasaia sula*	U.S.
14	Yojoa Scrub-Hairstreak, *Strymon yojoa*	U.S.
15	Salt Marsh Skipper, *Panoquina panoquin*	U.S.
16	Polka-dotted Yellowmark, *Baeotis sulphurea*	Mexico
17	Beautiful Beamer, *Phocides belus*	Mexico
18	White-rayed Patch, *Chlosyne ehrenbergii*	Mexico
19	Crossline Skipper, *Polites origenes*	U.S.
20	Juno Heliconian (Silverspot), *Dione juno*	Mexico
21	Orange-spotted Skipper, *Atarnes sallei*	Mexico
22, 23	American Lady, *Vanessa virginiensis*	U.S.
24	Mulberry Wing, *Poanes massasoit*	U.S.
25	Mexican Bluewing, *Myscelia ethusa*	U.S.
26	Blue-and-black Skipper, *Paches loxus*	Mexico
27	Variable Cracker, *Hamadryas feronia*	Mexico
28	Brown Argus, *Aricia agestis*	Italy
29	White Eyemark, *Leucochimona vestalis*	Mexico

30	Orange Mapwing, *Hypanartia lethe*	Mexico
31	Blomfild's Beauty, *Smyrna blomfildia*	Mexico
32, 33	Ruddy Copper, *Lycaena rubidus*	U.S.
34	Whirlabout, *Polites vibex*	U.S.
35	Striped Hairstreak, *Satyrium liparops*	U.S.
36	Large Wall Brown, *Lasiommata maera*	Italy
37	Southern Festoon, *Zerynthia polyxena*	Italy
38	*Hamadryas chloe*	Peru
39	Green-backed Ruby-eye, *Perichares philetes*	Mexico
40	Gray Hairstreak, *Strymon melinus*	U.S.
41	Sky-blue Greatstreak, *Pseudolycaena damo*	Mexico
42–43	Great Spangled Fritillary, *Speyeria cybele*	U.S.
44	Black-patched Bluemark, *Lasaia agesilas*	Mexico
45	Gulf Fritillary, *Agraulis vanillae*	U.S.
46	Carousing Jewelmark, *Anteros carausius*	Mexico
47	Banded Peacock, *Anartia fatima*	Mexico
48, 49	Tropical Leafwing, *Anaea aidea*	Mexico
50–51	Black-bordered Tegosa, *Tegosa anieta*	Mexico
52	Square-spotted Yellowmark, *Baeotis zonata*	Mexico
53	Green-eyed White, *Leptophobia aripa*	Mexico
54	Square-tipped Crescent, *Eresia phillyra*	Mexico
55	Malachite, *Siproeta stelenes*	Mexico
56	Thick-tipped Greta, *Greta morgane*	Mexico
57	Simple Patch, *Chlosyne hippodrome*	Mexico
58	Sealpoint Metalmark, *Apodemia hypoglauca*	Mexico

59	Alana White-Skipper, *Heliopetes alana*	Mexico
60, 61	Eastern Tailed-Blue, *Everes comyntas*	U.S.
62	Blue-studded Skipper, *Sostrata bifasciata*	Mexico
63	*Mylon Jason*	Mexico
64	Dark Kite-Swallowtail, *Eurytides philolaus*	Mexico
65	Rayed Sister, *Adelpha melanthe*	Mexico
66	Thick-bordered Kite-Swallowtail, *Eurytides dioxippus*	Mexico
67	Mexican Dartwhite, *Catasticta nimbice*	Mexico
68	Many-banded Daggerwing, *Marpesia chiron*	Mexico
69	Disturbed Tigerwing, *Mechanitis polymnia*	Mexico
70	Delaware Skipper, *Anatrytone logan*	U.S.
71	Empress Leilia, *Asterocampa leilia*	U.S.
72	Celadon Sister, *Adelpha serpa celerio*	Mexico
73	Carousing Jewelmark, *Anteros carausius*	Mexico
74	Common Checkered-Skipper, *Pyrgus communis*	U.S.
75	Soldier, *Danaus eresimus*	U.S.
76	Anna's Eighty-eight, *Diaethria anna*	Mexico
77	'Turquoise-spotted' Navy Eighty-eight, *Diaethria astala astala*	Mexico
78	Hispaniolan Leafwing, *Anaea troglodyta*	Dominican Republic
79	Silver Emperor, *Doxocopa laure*	Mexico
80, 81	Banded Orange Heliconian, *Dryadula phaetusa*	Mexico
82	'Colima' Navy Eighty-eight, *Diaethria astala asteria*	Mexico
83	Common Banner, *Epiphile adrasta*	Mexico
84	Isabella's Heliconian, *Euiedes isabella*	Mexico

85	Westwood's Satyr, *Euptychia westwoodi*	Mexico
86	Black Swallowtail, *Papilio polyxenes*	U.S.
87	Sword-tailed Beautymark, *Rhetus arcius*	Mexico
88	Variable Cracker, *Hamadryas feronia*	Mexico
89	Klug's Clearwing, *Dircenna klugii*	Mexico
90	Purple-washed Eyemark, *Mesosemia tetrica*	Mexico
91	Common Catone, *Catonephele numilia*	Mexico
92, 93	White Peacock, *Anartia jatrophae*	U.S.
94	Zebra-crossing Hairstreak, *Pantheides bathildis*	Mexico
95	'Stella' Sara Orangetip, *Anthocharis sara stella*	U.S.
96	Black Swallowtail, *Papilio polyxenes*	U.S.
97	Lantana Scrub-Hairstreak, *Strymon bazochii*	Mexico
98	Small Heath, *Coenonympha pamphilus*	Italy
99	Italian Marbled White, *Melanargia arge*	Italy
100, 101	Swamp Metalmark, *Calephelis muticum*	N.A.
102	*Ipidecla miadora*	Mexico
103	Three-tailed Swallowtail, *Papilio pilumnus*	Mexico
104	Two-barred Flasher, *Astraptes fulgerator*	U.S.
105	White Morpho, *Morpho polyphemus*	Mexico
106	Eastern Tiger Swallowtail, *Papilio glaucus*	U.S.
107	Crossline Skipper, *Polites origenes*	U.S.
108	*Calisto confusa*	Dominican Republic
109	*Eurema pyro*	Dominican Republic
110	Sierra Sulphur, *Colias behrii*	U.S.
111	Superb Cycadian, *Eumaeus childrenae*	Mexico

112	Pearly Heath, *Coenonympha arcania*	Italy
113	Regal Greatstreak, *Evenus regalis*	Mexico
114, 115	American Snout, *Libytheana carinenta*	U.S.
116	Knapweed Fritillary, *Melitaea phoebe*	Italy
117	Red Cracker, *Hamadryas amphinome*	Mexico
118	*Ignata gadira*	Mexico
119	Banded Orange Heliconian, *Dryadula phaetusa*	Mexico
120	Yellow Angled-Sulphur, *Anteos maerula*	U.S.
121	Dorcas Copper, *Lycaena dorcas*	U.S.
122	Slaty Skipper, *Chiomara mithrax*	Mexico
123	Antillean Mimic-White, *Dismorphia spio*	Dominican Republic
124	Square-tipped Crescent, *Eresia phillyra*	Mexico
125	Mexican Cycadian, *Eumaeus toxea*	Mexico
126, 127	Blue-and-orange Eighty-eight, *Callicore tolima*	Mexico
128	One-spotted Prepona, *Prepona demophoon*	Dominican Republic
129	*Calisto franciscoi*	Mexico
130	Acadian Hairstreak, *Satyrium acadica*	U.S.
131	Behr's Hairstreak, *Satyrium behrii*	U.S.
132	Square-spotted Yellowmark, *Baeotis zonata*	Mexico
133	Bartram's Scrub-Hairstreak, *Strymon acis*	Dominican Republic
134	Superb Cycadian, *Eumaeus childrenae*	Mexico
135	Lilac-bordered Copper, *Lycaena nivalis*	U.S.
136	Sulphurs (Whites and Yellows), *Phoebis*	Mexico
137	*Pyrgus crisia*	Dominican Republic
138	Mallow Scrub-Hairstreak, *Strymon istapa*	Dominican Republic

139	Adonis Blue, *Lysandra bellargus*	Italy
140, 141	Malachite, *Siproeta stelenes*	Mexico
142	*Tmolus crolinus*	Mexico
143	Escher's Blue, *Agrodiaetus escheri*	Italy
144	Yellow-rimmed Eighty-eight, *Callicore texa*	Mexico
145	Elban Heath, *Coenonympha elbana*	Italy
146	Orange Tip, *Anthocharis cardamines*	Italy
147	Marsh Fritillary, *Euphydryas aurinia*	Italy
148, 149	Wavy-lined Sunstreak, *Arcas cypria*	Mexico
150	Sword-tailed Beautymark, *Rhetus arcius*	Mexico
151	White-posted Metalmark, *Calosiama lilina*	Mexico
152	Adonis Blue, *Lysandra bellargus*	Italy
153	Small Heath, *Coenonympha pamphilus*	Italy
154	Green-veined White, *Pieris napi*	Italy
155	Marsh Fritillary, *Euphydryas aurinia*	Italy
156	Anna's Eighty-eight, *Diaethria anna*	Mexico
157	Italian Marbled White, *Melanargia arge*	Italy
158	Guatemalan Patch, *Chlosyne erodyle*	Mexico
159	Salvin's Ticlear, *Episcada salvinia*	Mexico
160, 161	Dingy Purplewing, *Eunica monima*	Mexico
162	Blue-eyed Sailor, *Dynamine dyonis*	Mexico
163	Simple Patch, *Chlosyne hippodrome*	Mexico
164	White-edged Red-ring, *Pyrrhogyra otolais*	Mexico
165	Juno Heliconian (Silverspot), *Dione juno*	Mexico
166, 167	Golden Melwhite, *Melete polyhymnia*	Mexico

168	Tailed Copper, *Lycaena arota*	U.S.
169	Mexican Cycadian, *Eumaeus toxea*	Mexico
170	Theona Checkerspot, *Chlosyne theona*	Mexico
171	Glanville Fritillary, *Melitaea cinxia*	Italy
172	Orange Banner, *Temenis laothoe*	Mexico
173	Anna's Eighty-eight, *Diaethria anna*	Mexico
174, 175	Red Cracker, *Hamadryas amphinome*	Mexico
176	Fine-lined Stripe-streak, *Arawacus sito*	Mexico
177	Erato Heliconian, *Heliconius erato*	Mexico
178	Goodson's Greenstreak, *Cyanophrys goodsoni*	Mexico
179	Variable Cracker, *Hamadryas feronia*	Mexico
180	*Erora carla*	Mexico
181	Banded Peacock, *Anartia fatima*	Mexico
182	Erato Heliconian, *Heliconius erato*	Mexico
183	Many-banded Daggerwing, *Marpesia chiron*	Mexico
184	Brownish Cracker, *Hamadryas iphthime*	Mexico
185	Disturbed Tigerwing, *Mechanitis polymnia*	Mexico
186–187	Common Wood-Nymph, *Cercyonis pegala*	U.S.
188	Aztec Skipper, *Cycloglypha thrasibulus*	Mexico
189	Regal Greatstreak, *Evenus regalis*	Mexico
190	Klug's Clearwing, *Dircenna klugii*	Mexico
191	Bow-lined Kite-Swallowtail, *Eurytides macrosilaus*	Mexico
192	Black-patched Bluemark, *Lasaia agesilas*	Mexico
193	*Thereus cithonius*	Mexico
194	Simple Patch, *Chlosyne hippodrome*	Mexico

195	Mother-of-Pearl Hairstreak, *Rekoa meton*	Mexico
196–197	Olympia Marble, *Euchloe olympia*	U.S.
198	Palamedes Swallowtail, *Papilio palamedes*	U.S.
199	Double-striped Longtail, *Urbanus belli*	Mexico
200	Fox-face Lemmark, *Thisbe lycorias*	Mexico
201	*Parrhasius orgia*	Mexico
202	Lowland Owlet, *Opsiphanes invirae*	Mexico
203	Curve-lined Theope, *Theope bacenis*	Mexico
204, 205	Orange Sulphur, *Colias eurytheme*	U.S.
206	Fatal Metalmark, *Calephelis nemesis*	U.S.
207	Androgeus Swallowtail, *Papilio androgeus*	Mexico
208	Sword-tailed Beautymark, *Rhetus arcius*	Mexico
209	Spineless Silverdrop, *Epargyreus aspina*	Mexico
210	De la Maza's Mimic-White, *Enantia mazai*	Mexico
211	*Pierids*	Mexico
212	Longtail sp., *Urbanus* sp.	Mexico
213	Common Streaky-Skipper, *Celotes nessus*	U.S.
214, 215	Eastern Tiger Swallowtail, *Papilio glaucus*	U.S.
216	Tiger Heliconian, *Heliconius ismenius*	Mexico
217	Oak Hairstreak, *Satyrium favonius*	U.S.
218	Two-barred Flasher, *Astraptes fulgerator*	U.S.
219	Crimson Patch, *Chlosyne janais*	Mexico
220, 221	Dual-spotted Swallowtail, *Mimoides ilus*	Mexico
222	Definite Patch, *Chlosyne definita*	U.S.
223	Zilpa Longtail, *Chioides zilpa*	U.S.

224	Desert Checkered-Skipper, *Pyrgus philetas*	U.S.
225	Sword-tailed Beautymark, *Rhetus arcius*	Mexico
226	Red-bordered Pixie, *Melanis pixe*	U.S.
227	Common Mestra, *Mestra amymone*	U.S.
228, 229	Mexican Silverspot, *Dione moneta*	U.S.
230–231	Tailed Orange, *Eurema proterpia*	U.S.
232	Fiery Skipper, *Hylephila phyleus*	U.S.
233	Silver-spotted Skipper, *Epargyreus clarus*	U.S.
234	Erato Heliconian, *Heliconius erato*	Mexico
235	Tailed Orange, *Eurema proterpia*	U.S.
236, 237	Baltimore Checkerspot, *Euphydryas phaeton*	U.S.
238	Orange-barred Sulphur, *Phoebis philea*	U.S.
239	Little Wood-Satyr, *Megisto cymela*	U.S.
240	Orange-bordered Firetip, *Pyrrhopyge chloris*	Mexico
241	Erichson's White-Skipper, *Heliopetes domicella*	U.S.
242	Common Buckeye, *Junonia coenia*	U.S.
243	Black Swallowtail, *Papilio polyxenes*	U.S.
244, 245	Eyed Brown, *Satyrodes eurydice*	U.S.
246	Bordered Patch, *Chlosyne lacinia*	U.S.
247	Southern Dogface, *Colias cesonia*	U.S.
248	Florida Purplewing, *Eunica tatila*	U.S.
249	Cyan Bluewing, *Myscelia cyaniris*	Mexico
250	Gilbert's Flasher, *Astraptes gilberti*	Mexico
251	Gray Cracker, *Hamadryas februa*	Mexico
252	Coronis Fritillary, *Speyeria coronis*	U.S.

253	Yellow-spotted Swallowtail, *Battus laodamus*	Mexico
254, 255	Clouded Sulphur, *Colias philodice*	U.S.
256	Tawny Emperor, *Asterocampa clyton*	U.S.
257	Black Swallowtail, *Papilio polyxenes*	U.S.
258	*Ipidecla schausi*	Mexico
259	Tawny Emperor, *Asterocampa clyton*	U.S.
260	Chiapas Stripe-streak, *Arawacus togarna*	Mexico
261	Regal Greatstreak, *Evenus regalis*	Mexico
262	Sky-blue Greatstreak, *Pseudolycaena damo*	Mexico
263	Silver-banded Hairstreak, *Chlorostrymon simaethis*	Mexico
264–265	Silver-spotted Skipper, *Epargyreus clarus*	U.S.
266	White-spotted Greatstreak, *Atlides carpasia*	Mexico
267	Large Orange Sulphur, *Phoebis agarithe*	U.S.
268	Empress Leilia, *Asterocampa leilia*	U.S.
269	Scintillant sp., *Calephelis* sp.	Mexico
270	Black Hairstreak, *Ocaria ocrisia*	Mexico
271	Sickle-winged Skipper, *Achlyodes thraso*	U.S.
272	Dina Yellow, *Eurema dina*	Mexico
273	Smoky Mylon, *Mylon zephus*	Mexico
274	Clytie Ministreak, *Ministrymon clytie*	Mexico
275	Guatemalan Geomark, *Mesene croceella*	Mexico
276	Common Wood-Nymph, *Cercyonis pegala*	U.S.
277	Oak Hairstreak, *Satyrium favonius*	U.S.
278	Mexican Mottlemark, *Calydna sinuata*	Mexico
279	Theona Checkerspot, *Chlosyne theona*	Mexico

280	Blue-and-black Skipper, *Paches loxus*	Mexico
281	Yojoa Scrub-Hairstreak, *Strymon yojoa*	U.S.
282, 283	*Lamprospilus collucia*	Mexico
284	Delaware Skipper, *Anatrytone logan*	U.S.
285	White Peacock, *Anartia jatrophae*	U.S.
286	Common Buckeye, *Junonia coenia*	U.S.
287	Lamplight Actinote, *Altinote ozomene*	U.S.
288	Holy Leafwing, *Zaretis ellops*	U.S.
289	Pearl Crescent, *Phyciodes tharos*	U.S.
290–291	Gulf Fritillary, *Agraulis vanillae*	U.S.
292	Red-spotted Purple, *Limenitis arthemis astyanax*	U.S.
293	Sulphurs (Whites and Yellows), *Phoebis*	Mexico
294	Hessel's Hairstreak, *Callophrys hesseli*	U.S.
295	Sharp Banded-Skipper, *Autochton zarex*	U.S.
296–297	Malachite, *Siproeta stelenes*	U.S.
298	American Lady, *Vanessa virginiensis*	U.S.
299	Tailed Orange, *Eurema proterpia*	U.S.

Index of Common and Scientific Names of Butterflies

Each butterfly is listed in the index twice: once by its common name and again by its scientific name. The location indicates where the photograph of the butterfly was taken.

Butterfly	Location	Page
Acadian Hairstreak, *Satyrium acadica*	U.S.	130
Achlyodes thraso, Sickle-winged Skipper	U.S.	271
Adelpha serpa celerio, Celadon Sister	Mexico	72
Adelpha melanthe, Rayed Sister	Mexico	65
Adonis Blue, *Lysandra bellargus*	Italy	139, 152
Agraulis vanillae, Gulf Fritillary	U.S.	45, 290-291
Agrodiaetus escheri, Escher's Blue	Italy	143
Alana White-Skipper, *Heliopetes alana*	Mexico	59
Altinote ozomene, Lamplight Actinote	U.S.	287
American Lady, *Vanessa virginiensis*	U.S.	22, 23, 298
American Snout, *Libytheana carinenta*	U.S.	114, 115
Anaea aidea, Tropical Leafwing	Mexico	48, 49
Anaea troglodyta, Hispaniolan Leafwing	Dominican Republic	78
Anartia fatima, Banded Peacock	Mexico	47, 181
Anartia jatrophae, White Peacock	U.S.	92, 93, 285
Anatrytone logan, Delaware Skipper	U.S.	70, 284
Androgeus Swallowtail, *Papilio androgeus*	Mexico	207

Anna's Eighty-eight, *Diaethria anna*	Mexico	76, 156, 173
Anteos maerula, Yellow Angled-Sulphur	U.S.	120
Anteros carausius, Carousing Jewelmark	Mexico	46, 73
Anthocharis cardamines, Orange Tip	Italy	146
Anthocharis sara stella, 'Stella' Sara Orangetip	U.S.	95
Antillean Mimic-White, *Dismorphia spio*	Dominican Republic	123
Altinote ozomene, Lamplight Actinote	U.S.	287
Apodemia hypoglauca, Sealpoint Metalmark	Mexico	58
Arawacus sito, Fine-lined Stripe-streak	Mexico	176
Arawacus togarna, Chiapas Stripe-streak	Mexico	260
Arcas cypria, Wavy-lined Sunstreak	Mexico	148, 149
Aricia agestis, Brown Argus	Italy	28
Asterocampa clyton, Tawny Emperor	U.S.	256, 259
Asterocampa leilia, Empress Leilia	U.S.	71, 268
Astraptes fulgerator, Two-barred Flasher	U.S.	104, 218
Astraptes gilberti, Gilbert's Flasher	Mexico	250
Atarnes sallei, Orange-spotted Skipper	Mexico	21
Atlides carpasia, White-spotted Greatstreak	Mexico	266
Autochton zarex, Sharp Banded-Skipper	U.S.	295
Aztec Skipper, *Cycloglypha thrasibulus*	Mexico	188
Baeotis sulphurea, Polka-dotted Yellowmark	Mexico	16
Baeotis zonata, Square-spotted Yellowmark	Mexico	52, 132
Baltimore Checkerspot, *Euphydryas phaeton*	U.S.	236, 237
Banded Orange Heliconian, *Dryadula phaetusa*	Mexico	80, 81, 119

Banded Peacock, *Anartia fatima*	Mexico	47, 181
Bartram's Scrub-Hairstreak, *Strymon acis*	Dominican Republic	133
Battus laodamus, Yellow-spotted Swallowtail	Mexico	253
Beautiful Beamer, *Phocides belus*	Mexico	17
Behr's Hairstreak, *Satyrium behrii*	U.S.	131
Black-bordered Tegosa, *Tegosa anieta*	Mexico	50-51
Black-patched Bluemark, *Lasaia agesilas*	Mexico	44, 192
Black Hairstreak, *Ocaria ocrisia*	Mexico	270
Black Swallowtail, *Papilio polyxenes*	U.S.	86, 96, 243, 257
Blomfild's Beauty, *Smyrna blomfildia*	Mexico	31
Blue-and-black Skipper, *Paches loxus*	Mexico	26, 280
Blue-and-orange Eighty-eight, *Callicore tolima*	Mexico	126, 127
Blue-eyed Sailor, *Dynamine dyonis*	Mexico	162
Blue Metalmark, *Lasaia sula*	U.S.	13
Blue-studded Skipper, *Sostrata bifasciata*	Mexico	62
Bordered Patch, *Chlosyne lacinia*	U.S.	246
Bow-lined Kite-Swallowtail, *Eurytides macrosilaus*	Mexico	191
Brown Argus, *Aricia agestis*	Italy	28
Brownish Cracker, *Hamadryas iphthime*	Mexico	184
Calephelis sp., Scintillant sp.	Mexico	269
Calephelis muticum, Swamp Metalmark	U.S.	100, 101
Calephelis nemesis, Fatal Metalmark	U.S.	206
Calisto confusa	Dominican Republic	108

Calisto franciscoi — Mexico — 129
Callicore texa, Yellow-rimmed Eighty-eight — Mexico — 144
Callicore tolima, Blue-and-orange Eighty-eight — Mexico — 126, 127
Callophrys hesseli, Hessel's Hairstreak — U.S. — 294
Calosiama lilina, White-posted Metalmark — Mexico — 151
Calydna sinuata, Mexican Mottlemark — Mexico — 278
Carousing Jewelmark, *Anteros carausius* — Mexico — 46, 73
Catasticta nimbice, Mexican Dartwhite — Mexico — 67
Catonephele numilia, Common Catone — Mexico — 91
Celadon Sister, *Adelpha serpa celerio* — Mexico — 72
Celotes nessus, Common Streaky-Skipper — U.S. — 213
Cercyonis pegala, Common Wood-Nymph — U.S. — 186-187, 276
Chiapas Stripe-streak, *Arawacus togarna* — Mexico — 260
Chioides zilpa, Zilpa Longtail — U.S. — 223
Chiomara mithrax, Slaty Skipper — Mexico — 122
Chlorostrymon simaethis,
  Silver-banded Hairstreak — Mexico — 263
Chlosyne definita, Definite Patch — U.S. — 222
Chlosyne ehrenbergii, White-rayed Patch — Mexico — 18
Chlosyne erodyle, Guatemalan Patch — Mexico — 158
Chlosyne hippodrome, Simple Patch — Mexico — 57, 163, 194
Chlosyne janais, Crimson Patch — Mexico — 219
Chlosyne lacinia, Bordered Patch — U.S. — 246
Chlosyne theona, Theona Checkerspot — Mexico — 170, 279
Clouded Sulphur, *Colias philodice* — U.S. — 254, 255

Clytie Ministreak, *Ministrymon clytie* — Mexico — 274
Coenonympha arcania, Pearly Heath — Italy — 112
Coenonympha elbana, Elban Heath — Italy — 145
Coenonympha pamphilus, Small Heath — Italy — 98, 153
Colias behrii, Sierra Sulphur — U.S. — 110
Colias cesonia, Southern Dogface — U.S. — 10, 11, 247
Colias eurytheme, Orange Sulphur — U.S. — 204, 205
Colias philodice, Clouded Sulphur — U.S. — 254, 255
'Colima' Navy Eighty-eight, *Diaethria astala asteria* — Mexico — 82
Common Banner, *Epiphile adrasta* — Mexico — 83
Common Buckeye, *Junonia coenia* — U.S. — 242, 286
Common Catone, *Catonephele numilia* — Mexico — 91
Common Checkered-Skipper, *Pyrgus communis* — U.S. — 74
Common Mestra, *Mestra amymone* — U.S. — 227
Common Streaky-Skipper, *Celotes nessus* — U.S. — 213
Common Wood-Nymph, *Cercyonis pegala* — U.S. — 186-187, 276
Coronis Fritillary, *Speyeria coronis* — U.S. — 252
Crimson Patch, *Chlosyne janais* — Mexico — 219
Crossline Skipper, *Polites origenes* — U.S. — 19, 107
Curve-lined Theope, *Theope bacenis* — Mexico — 203
Cyan Bluewing, *Myscelia cyaniris* — Mexico — 249
Cyanophrys goodsoni, Goodson's Greenstreak — Mexico — 178
Cycloglypha thrasibulus, Aztec Skipper — Mexico — 188

Danaus eresimus, Soldier	U.S.	75
Danaus gilippus, Queen	Dominican Republic	8
Dark Kite-Swallowtail, *Eurytides philolaus*	Mexico	64
Definite Patch, *Chlosyne definita*	U.S.	222
De la Maza's Mimic-White, *Enantia mazai*	Mexico	210
Delaware Skipper, *Anatrytone logan*	U.S.	70, 284
Desert Checkered-Skipper, *Pyrgus philetas*	U.S.	224
Diaethria anna, Anna's Eighty-eight	Mexico	76, 156, 173
Diaethria astala astala, 'Turquoise-spotted' Navy Eighty-eight	Mexico	77
Diaethria astala asteria, 'Colima' Navy Eighty-eight	Mexico	82
Dina Yellow, *Eurema dina*	Mexico	272
Dingy Purplewing, *Eunica monima*	Mexico	160, 161
Dione juno, Juno Heliconian (Silverspot)	Mexico	20, 165
Dione moneta, Mexican Silverspot	U.S.	228, 229
Dircenna klugii, Klug's Clearwing	Mexico	89, 190
Dismorphia spio, Antillean Mimic-White	Dominican Republic	123
Disturbed Tigerwing, *Mechanitis polymnia*	Mexico	69, 185
Dorcas Copper, *Lycaena dorcas*	U.S.	121
Double-striped Longtail, *Urbanus belli*	Mexico	199
Doxocopa laure, Silver Emperor	Mexico	79
Dryadula phaetusa, Banded Orange Heliconian	Mexico	80, 81, 119
Dual-spotted Swallowtail, *Mimoides ilus*	Mexico	220, 221
Dynamine dyonis, Blue-eyed Sailor	Mexico	162

Eastern Tailed-Blue, *Everes comyntas*   U.S.   60, 61
Eastern Tiger Swallowtail, *Papilio glaucus*   U.S.   106, 214, 215
Elban Heath, *Coenonympha elbana*   Italy   145
Empress Leilia, *Asterocampa leilia*   U.S.   71, 268
Enantia mazai, De la Maza's Mimic-White   Mexico   210
Epargyreus aspina, Spineless Silverdrop   Mexico   209
Epargyreus clarus, Silver-spotted Skipper   U.S.   233, 264-265
Epiphile adrasta, Common Banner   Mexico   83
Episcada salvinia, Salvin's Ticlear   Mexico   159
Erato Heliconian, *Heliconius erato*   Mexico   177, 182, 234
Eresia phillyra, Square-tipped Crescent   Mexico   54, 124
Erichson's White-Skipper, *Heliopetes domicella*   U.S.   241
Erora carla   Mexico   180
Escher's Blue, *Agrodiaetus escheri*   Italy   143
Euchloe olympia, Olympia Marble   U.S.   196-197
Euiedes isabella, Isabella's Heliconian   Mexico   84
Eumaeus childrenae, Superb Cycadian   Mexico   111, 134
Eumaeus toxea, Mexican Cycadian   Mexico   125, 169
Eunica monima, Dingy Purplewing   Mexico   160, 161
Eunica tatila, Florida Purplewing   U.S.   248
Euphydryas aurinia, Marsh Fritillary   Italy   147, 155
Euphydryas phaeton, Baltimore Checkerspot   U.S.   236, 237
Euptychia westwoodi, Westwood's Satyr   Mexico   85
Eurema dina, Dina Yellow   Mexico   272
Eurema proterpia, Tailed Orange   U.S.   230-231, 235, 299

Eurema pyro	Dominican Republic	109
Eurytides dioxippus, Thick-bordered Kite-Swallowtail	Mexico	66
Eurytides macrosilaus, Bow-lined Kite Swallowtail	Mexico	191
Eurytides philolaus, Dark Kite-Swallowtail	Mexico	64
Evenus regalis, Regal Greatstreak	Mexico	113, 189, 261
Everes comyntas, Eastern Tailed-Blue	Mexico	60, 61
Eyed Brown, *Satyrodes eurydice*	U.S.	244, 245
Fatal Metalmark, *Calephelis nemesis*	U.S.	206
Fiery Skipper, *Hylephila phyleus*	U.S.	232
Fine-lined Stripe-streak, *Arawacus sito*	Mexico	176
Florida Purplewing, *Eunica tatila*	U.S.	248
Fox-face Lemmark, *Thisbe lycorias*	Mexico	200
Gilbert's Flasher, *Astraptes gilberti*	Mexico	250
Glanville Fritillary, *Melitaea cinxia*	Italy	171
Golden Melwhite, *Melete polyhymnia*	Mexico	166, 167
Goodson's Greenstreak, *Cyanophrys goodsoni*	Mexico	178
Gray Cracker, *Hamadryas februa*	Mexico	251
Gray Hairstreak, *Strymon melinus*	U.S.	40
Green-backed Ruby-eye, *Perichares philetes*	Mexico	39
Green-eyed White, *Leptophobia aripa*	Mexico	53
Green-veined White, *Pieris napi*	Italy	154

Great Spangled Fritillary, *Speyeria cybele*	U.S.	42-43
Greta morgane, Thick-tipped Greta	Mexico	56
Guatemalan Geomark, *Mesene croceella*	Mexico	275
Guatemalan Patch, *Chlosyne erodyle*	Mexico	158
Gulf Fritillary, *Agraulis vanillae*	U.S.	45, 290-291
Hamadryas amphinome, Red Cracker	Mexico	117, 174, 175
Hamadryas chloe	Peru	38
Hamadryas februa, Gray Cracker	Mexico	251
Hamadryas feronia, Variable Cracker	Mexico	27, 88, 179
Hamadryas iphthime, Brownish Cracker	Mexico	184
Heliconius charithonia, Zebra Heliconian	U.S.	12
Heliconius erato, Erato Heliconian	Mexico	177, 182, 234
Heliconius ismenius, Tiger Heliconian	Mexico	216
Heliopetes alana, Alana White-Skipper	Mexico	59
Heliopetes domicella, Erichson's White-Skipper	U.S.	241
Hessel's Hairstreak, *Callophrys hesseli*	U.S.	294
Hispaniolan Leafwing, *Anaea troglodyta*	Dominican Republic	78
Holy Leafwing, *Zaretis ellops*	U.S.	288
Hylephila phyleus, Fiery Skipper	U.S.	232
Hypanartia lethe, Orange Mapwing	Mexico	30
Ignata gadira	Mexico	118
Ipidecla miadora	Mexico	102
Ipidecla schausi	Mexico	258

Isabella's Heliconian, *Euiedes isabella*	Mexico	84
Italian Marbled White, *Melanargia arge*	Italy	99, 157
Junonia coenia, Common Buckeye	U.S.	242, 286
Juno Heliconian (Silverspot), *Dione juno*	Mexico	20, 165
Klug's Clearwing, *Dircenna klugii*	Mexico	89, 190
Knapweed Fritillary, *Melitaea phoebe*	Italy	116
Lamplight Actinote, *Altinote ozomene*	U.S.	287
Lamprospilus collucia	Mexico	282, 283
Lantana Scrub-Hairstreak, *Strymon bazochii*	Mexico	97
Large Orange Sulphur, *Phoebis agarithe*	U.S.	267
Large Wall Brown, *Lasiommata maera*	Italy	36
Lasaia agesilas, Black-patched Bluemark	Mexico	44, 192
Lasaia sula, Blue Metalmark	U.S.	13
Lasiommata maera, Large Wall Brown	Italy	36
Leptophobia aripa, Green-eyed White	Mexico	53
Leucochimona vestalis, White Eyemark	Mexico	29
Libytheana carinenta, American Snout	U.S.	114, 115
Lilac-bordered Copper, *Lycaena nivalis*	U.S.	135
Limenitis arthemis astyanax, Red-spotted Purple	U.S.	292
Little Wood-Satyr, *Megisto cymela*	U.S.	239
Longtail sp., *Urbanus* sp.	Mexico	212
Lowland Owlet, *Opsiphanes invirae*	Mexico	202

Lycaena arota, Tailed Copper	U.S.	168
Lycaena dorcas, Dorcas Copper	U.S.	121
Lycaena nivalis, Lilac-bordered Copper	U.S.	135
Lycaena rubidus, Ruddy Copper	U.S.	32, 33
Lysandra bellargus, Adonis Blue	Italy	139, 152
Malachite, *Siproeta stelenes*	Mexico	55, 140, 141, 296-297
Mallow Scrub-Hairstreak, *Strymon istapa*	Dominican Republic	138
Many-banded Daggerwing, *Marpesia chiron*	Mexico	68, 183
Marpesia chiron, Many-banded Daggerwing	Mexico	68, 183
Marsh Fritillary, *Euphydryas aurinia*	Italy	147, 155
Mechanitis polymnia, Disturbed Tigerwing	Mexico	69, 185
Megisto cymela, Little Wood-Satyr	U.S.	239
Melanargia arge, Italian Marbled White	Italy	99, 157
Melanis cephise, White-rayed Pixie	Mexico	9
Melanis pixe, Red-bordered Pixie	U.S.	226
Melete polyhymnia, Golden Melwhite	Mexico	166, 167
Melitaea cinxia, Glanville Fritillary	Italy	171
Melitaea phoebe, Knapweed Fritillary	Italy	116
Mesene croceella, Guatemalan Geomark	Mexico	275
Mesosemia tetrica, Purple-washed Eyemark	Mexico	90
Mestra amymone, Common Mestra	U.S.	227
Mexican Bluewing, *Myscelia ethusa*	U.S.	25
Mexican Cycadian, *Eumaeus toxea*	Mexico	125, 169
Mexican Dartwhite, *Catasticta nimbice*	Mexico	67

Mexican Mottlemark, *Calydna sinuata* — Mexico — 278
Mexican Silverspot, *Dione moneta* — U.S. — 228, 229
Mimoides ilus, Dual-spotted Swallowtail — Mexico — 220, 221
Ministrymon clytie, Clytie Ministreak — Mexico — 274
Morpho polyphemus, White Morpho — Mexico — 105
Mother-of-Pearl Hairstreak, *Rekoa meton* — Mexico — 195
Mulberry Wing, *Poanes massasoit* — U.S. — 24
Mylon Jason — Mexico — 63
Mylon zephus, Smoky Mylon — Mexico — 273
Myscelia cyaniris, Cyan Bluewing — Mexico — 249
Myscelia ethusa, Mexican Bluewing — U.S. — 25

Oak Hairstreak, *Satyrium favonius* — U.S. — 217, 277
Ocaria ocrisia, Black Hairstreak — Mexico — 270
Olympia Marble, *Euchloe olympia* — U.S. — 196-197
One-spotted Prepona, *Prepona demophoon* — Dominican Republic — 128
Opsiphanes invirae, Lowland Owlet — Mexico — 202
Orange Banner, *Temenis laothoe* — Mexico — 172
Orange-barred Sulphur, *Phoebis philea* — U.S. — 238
Orange-bordered Firetip, *Pyrrhopyge chloris* — Mexico — 240
Orange Mapwing, *Hypanartia lethe* — Mexico — 30
Orange-spotted Skipper, *Atarnes sallei* — Mexico — 21
Orange Sulphur, *Colias eurytheme* — U.S. — 204, 205
Orange Tip, *Anthocharis cardamines* — Italy — 146

Paches loxus, Blue-and-black Skipper	Mexico	26, 280
Palamedes Swallowtail, *Papilio palamedes*	U.S.	198
Panoquina panoquin, Salt Marsh Skipper	U.S.	15
Pantheides bathildis, Zebra-crossing Hairstreak	Mexico	94
Papilio androgeus, Androgeus Swallowtail	Mexico	207
Papilio glaucus, Eastern Tiger Swallowtail	U.S.	106, 214, 215
Papilio palamedes, Palamedes Swallowtail	U.S.	198
Papilio pilumnus, Three-tailed Swallowtail	Mexico	103
Papilio polyxenes, Black Swallowtail	U.S.	86, 96, 243, 257
Parrhasius orgia	Mexico	201
Pearl Crescent, *Phyciodes tharos*	U.S.	289
Pearly Heath, *Coenonympha arcania*	Italy	112
Perichares philetes, Green-backed Ruby-eye	Mexico	39
Phocides belus, Beautiful Beamer	Mexico	17
Phoebis, Sulphurs (Whites and Yellows)	Mexico	136, 293
Phoebis agarithe, Large Orange Sulphur	U.S.	267
Phoebis philea, Orange-barred Sulphur	U.S.	238
Phyciodes tharos, Pearl Crescent	U.S.	289
Pierids	Mexico	211
Pieris napi, Green-veined White	Italy	154
Poanes massasoit, Mulberry Wing	U.S.	24
Polites origenes, Crossline Skipper	U.S.	19, 107
Polites vibex, Whirlabout	U.S.	34
Polka-dotted Yellowmark, *Baeotis sulphurea*	Mexico	16
Prepona demophoon, One-spotted Prepona	Dominican Republic	128

Pseudolycaena damo, Sky-blue Greatstreak	Mexico	41, 262
Purple-washed Eyemark, *Mesosemia tetrica*	Mexico	90
Pyrgus communis, Common Checkered-Skipper	U.S.	74
Pyrgus crisia	Dominican Republic	137
Pyrgus philetas, Desert Checkered-Skipper	U.S.	224
Pyrrhogyra otolais, White-edged Red-ring	Mexico	164
Pyrrhopyge chloris, Orange-bordered Firetip	Mexico	240
Queen, *Danaus gilippus*	Dominican Republic	8
Rayed Sister, *Adelpha melanthe*	Mexico	65
Red-bordered Pixie, *Melanis pixe*	U.S.	226
Red Cracker, *Hamadryas amphinome*	Mexico	117, 174, 175
Red-spotted Purple, *Limenitis arthemis astyanax*	U.S.	292
Regal Greatstreak, *Evenus regalis*	Mexico	113, 189, 261
Rekoa meton, Mother-of-Pearl Hairstreak	Mexico	195
Rhetus arcius, Sword-tailed Beautymark	Mexico	87, 150, 208, 225
Ruddy Copper, *Lycaena rubidus*	U.S.	32, 33
Salt Marsh Skipper, *Panoquina panoquin*	U.S.	15
Salvin's Ticlear, *Episcada salvinia*	Mexico	159
Satyrium acadica, Acadian Hairstreak	U.S.	130
Satyrium behrii, Behr's Hairstreak	U.S.	131
Satyrium favonius, Oak Hairstreak	U.S.	217, 277
Satyrium liparops, Striped Hairstreak	U.S.	35

Satyrodes eurydice, Eyed Brown	U.S.	244, 245
Scintillant sp., *Calephelis* sp.	Mexico	269
Sealpoint Metalmark, *Apodemia hypoglauca*	Mexico	58
Sharp Banded-Skipper, *Autochton zarex*	U.S.	295
Sickle-winged Skipper, *Achlyodes thraso*	U.S.	271
Sierra Sulphur, *Colias behrii*	U.S.	110
Silver-banded Hairstreak, *Chlorostrymon simaethis*	Mexico	263
Silver Emperor, *Doxocopa laure*	Mexico	79
Silverspot (Juno Heliconian), *Dione juno*	Mexico	20, 165
Silver-spotted Skipper, *Epargyreus clarus*	U.S.	233, 264-265
Simple Patch, *Chlosyne hippodrome*	Mexico	57, 163, 194
Siproeta stelenes, Malachite	Mexico	55, 140, 141, 296-297
Sky-blue Greatstreak, *Pseudolycaena damo*	Mexico	41, 262
Slaty Skipper, *Chiomara mithrax*	Mexico	122
Small Heath, *Coenonympha pamphilus*	Italy	98, 153
Smoky Mylon, *Mylon zephus*	Mexico	273
Smyrna blomfildia, Blomfild's Beauty	Mexico	31
Soldier, *Danaus eresimus*	U.S.	75
Sostrata bifasciata, Blue-studded Skipper	Mexico	62
Southern Dogface, *Colias cesonia*	U.S.	10, 11, 247
Southern Festoon, *Zerynthia polyxena*	Italy	37
Speyeria coronis, Coronis Fritillary	U.S.	252
Speyeria cybele, Great Spangled Fritillary	U.S.	42-43
Spineless Silverdrop, *Epargyreus aspina*	Mexico	209
Square-spotted Yellowmark, *Baeotis zonata*	Mexico	52, 132

Square-tipped Crescent, *Eresia phillyra*	Mexico	54, 124
'Stella' Sara Orangetip, *Anthocharis sara stella*	U.S.	95
Striped Hairstreak, *Satyrium liparops*	U.S.	35
Strymon acis, Bartram's Scrub-Hairstreak	Dominican Republic	133
Strymon bazochii, Lantana Scrub-Hairstreak	Mexico	97
Strymon istapa, Mallow Scrub-Hairstreak	Dominican Republic	138
Strymon melinus, Gray Hairstreak	U.S.	40
Strymon yojoa, Yojoa Scrub-Hairstreak	U.S.	14, 281
Sulphurs (Whites and Yellows), *Phoebis*	Mexico	136, 293
Superb Cycadian, *Eumaeus childrenae*	Mexico	111, 134
Swamp Metalmark, *Calephelis muticum*	N.A.	100, 101
Sword-tailed Beautymark, *Rhetus arcius*	Mexico	87, 150, 208, 225
Tailed Copper, *Lycaena arota*	U.S.	168
Tailed Orange, *Eurema proterpia*	U.S.	230-231, 235, 299
Tawny Emperor, *Asterocampa clyton*	U.S.	256, 259
Tegosa anieta, Black-bordered Tegosa	Mexico	50-51
Temenis laothoe, Orange Banner	Mexico	172
Theona Checkerspot, *Chlosyne theona*	Mexico	170, 279
Theope bacenis, Curve-lined Theope	Mexico	203
Thereus cithonius	Mexico	193
Thick-bordered Kite-Swallowtail, *Eurytides dioxippus*	Mexico	66
Thick-tipped Greta, *Greta morgane*	Mexico	56

Thisbe lycorias, Fox-face Lemmark	Mexico	200
Three-tailed Swallowtail, *Papilio pilumnus*	Mexico	103
Tiger Heliconian, *Heliconius ismenius*	Mexico	216
Tmolus crolinus	Mexico	142
Tropical Leafwing, *Anaea aide*	Mexico	48, 49
'Turquoise-spotted' Navy Eighty-eight, *Diaethria astala astala*	Mexico	77
Two-barred Flasher, *Astraptes fulgerator*	U.S.	104, 218
Urbanus sp., Longtail sp.	Mexico	212
Urbanus belli, Double-striped Longtail	Mexico	199
Vanessa virginiensis, American Lady	U.S.	22, 23, 298
Variable Cracker, *Hamadryas feronia*	Mexico	27, 88, 179
Wavy-lined Sunstreak, *Arcas cypria*	Mexico	148, 149
Westwood's Satyr, *Euptychia westwoodi*	Mexico	85
Whirlabout, *Polites vibex*	U.S.	34
White-edged Red-ring, *Pyrrhogyra otolais*	Mexico	164
White Eyemark, *Leucochimona vestalis*	Mexico	29
White Morpho, *Morpho polyphemus*	Mexico	105
White Peacock, *Anartia jatrophae*	U.S.	92, 93, 285
White-posted Metalmark, *Calosiama lilina*	Mexico	151
White-rayed Patch, *Chlosyne ehrenbergii*	Mexico	18

White-rayed Pixie, *Melanis cephise*	Mexico	9
White-spotted Greatstreak, *Atlides carpasia*	Mexico	266
Yellow Angled-Sulphur, *Anteos maerula*	U.S.	120
Yellow-rimmed Eighty-eight, *Callicore texa*	Mexico	144
Yellow-spotted Swallowtail, *Battus laodamus*	Mexico	253
Yojoa Scrub-Hairstreak, *Strymon yojoa*	U.S.	14, 281
Zaretis ellops, Holy Leafwing	U.S.	288
Zebra-crossing Hairstreak, *Pantheides bathildis*	Mexico	94
Zebra Heliconian, *Heliconius charithonia*	U.S.	12
Zerynthia polyxena, Southern Festoon	Italy	37
Zilpa Longtail, *Chioides zilpa*	U.S.	223